THE ANIMAL RESCUE STORE

By
ELIZABETH SWADOS

Illustrated by
ANNE WILSON

ARTHUR A. LEVINE BOOKS • An Imprint of Scholastic Inc.

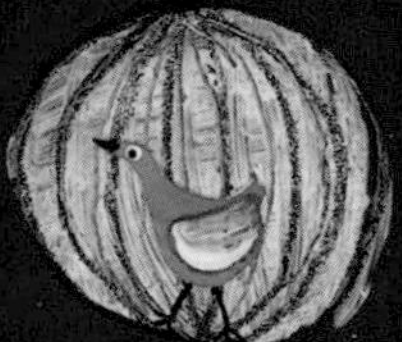

To Ruth Lichter and her beautiful daughter, Roz. – E.S.

For Simone and Rose with her wagging tail! – A.W.

Library of Congress Cataloging-in-Publication Data

Swados, Elizabeth.
The animal rescue store / by Elizabeth Swados ; illustrated by Anne Wilson. – 1st ed.
p. cm.
ISBN 0-439-55476-4
1. Animals—Juvenile poetry. 2. Animals—Treatment—Juvenile poetry.
3. Children's poetry, American. I. Wilson, Anne, 1974- II. Title.
PS3569.W17A84 2005
811'.54—dc22
2004005480

10 9 8 7 6 5 4 3 2 1 05 06 07 08 09

Book design by Elizabeth B. Parisi

First edition, March 2005 Printed in Singapore 46

This is a tribute to Buddy Shapiro and his store "Special Ts" on East 1st Street.

Table of Contents

Sidney's Store

Sidney's a man with a
Face like a clown's.
His nose hangs down and his eyes droop.
But he's an excited guy.
"Hello!" he shouts and shakes your hand.
"Hello!" he shouts and kisses your cheek.
"Hello!" He hugs you hard.
"Hello!" He'd bug you for a week.
Sidney's a friendly,
Soft-hearted guy.
Sidney's door is always open.

Hello hug
Handshake
Hello happy handshake hello.
He owns a pet store called Sidney's
(what else?)
"Hello baaybee.
You wanna pet
Maybe?"

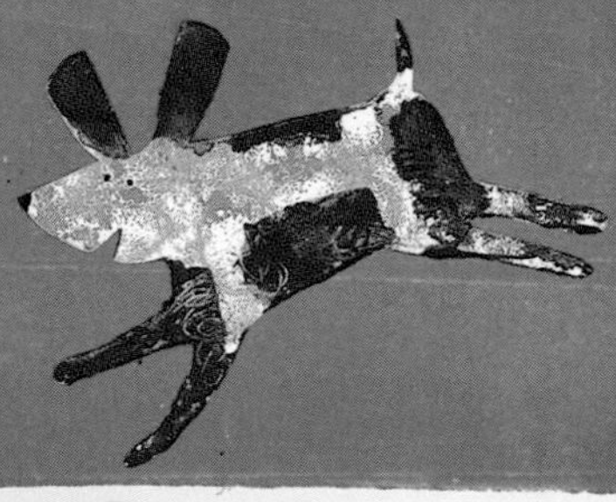

A special pet store. "Hello come in. Come in."
Unwanted animals
Abandoned pets
(Like when
A kid buys a pet
And forgets he has to
Feed it
Walk it
Clean it
You get it?)
"Hello come in," Sidney says.
"We got great news.
Baby alligators today.
Don't run away."
Hello hug handshakes hello.
Roar zzz chomp arf
Mrawoo yakka yakka!
"What did you say?
Can't hear you," says Sidney.

"Too many animals, my dear.
Today I found a nest of
Baby finches
Ouch! Their little beaks pinch!"
Sidney takes the strangest animals,
Heals them
And gives them away.
If he can't find a home for them
(Which is rare)
They just stay
And stay
Until they're bigger than him
And he can't find room
To sit down.
"Move over you little
Bear cub!"

OOPS!
Blub
Slurp
Goop
Badoop
Frowgd
Crawhk
Crawhk
Glurp
Frowgd
Croak
Croak
Glup

It's slithery up And slimy too. Oops it's over there!

Gotchoo!
Whoops gotcha again!
Whoops
Gotcha gotcha whoops!
Blurb slurb
Goop
Oopy
Doopy
Boops

FROG

Slithery boing
Boing boing
Oops gotcha!
Can't keep this oops oops slippery slimy
(Gotcha)
Guy in my hands.
Green slimy friend of mine
With stuck-out marble eyes,
We could have a real good time
Putting you in someone's
Shoe,
Dropping you down
Someone's back,
Laying you there
On someone's dish.
Under a pillow,
Under some sheets but
Just one thing . . .
Let's not get you
Squished.

F E R R E

The ferret's just
Fuzz with feet.
His nose is a raisin
That squishes and squeezes,
I'd take him home
But I think he'll
Cause sneezes.
Ahchoo Ahchoo Ahchoo!
Oh, what can I do?
Creatures with fur
Creatures that purr
Even smooth and bare
Animals
Make me Ahchoo. [sneezes occur]
Youch I feel prickles and itches
And cough! My throat tickles
And oow! My eyes swell
And nnnnk my nodes clodses. Ahhhchoo!
I'd like to tickle
This warm cuddly

T C H O O !

Circle of fur called a ferret,
But please take it away
Before I scare it
When my nose honks
And my lungs wheeze.
Yeah you've guessed it
I've got allergies.

Ahchoo. Ahchoo. Ahchoo.

Someone left a puppy
Awwwww
Someone left a wet puppy
Awwwww
Sweet fuzzy puppy
Awwwww
Lick lick lick
Puppy licks on my
Nose nuzzle puppy
Wet from the rain
Awwwww
Drip drip wet
Nuzzle me again.
Wet puppy drip puppy
Who would leave you
Tied here puppy?
Gonna take you home puppy.
Awwwww
C'mere puppy
Mine puppy
Waggle waggle
Tail like a fuzzy pinwheel
Awwwww
C'mere pal o' mine
Puppy.

Tabby

How 'bout me?
I'm a rough
Tumble tomboy tabby
Cat. Pssst!
I'm a crabby cat.
But a loyal cat.
I'm a scruffy cat.
Not no royal cat.
I don't go "meow."
I go
"MROW MROW."
Pssst! I fight in the street.
"POW POW POW"
I'm a strutter
From the gutter.
I'll steal your ham
And eat your butter, jam, or SPAM.
I'm proud of myself—don't you dig me! Psst!
I leap on the shelf.
Pizza watch out
I can't resist making a mess.
"MROW MROW MROW"

Hey I'm tough but also
I'm kind of kind
And I'll watch your behind.
My lives—I have nine.
I'm a gangsta with fur.
You might make me purr
If you find me a "her."
Purr Purr Purr.

Oh m'gosh stay away from
Me get that thing away from me
That yellow green slithering
Thing!
Oh it's slithering closer— get it
Away. It looks like a giant
Slimy shoelace
Put it down.
Are you putting it on
The ground no don't!
I don't like
I really don't like don't you don't you
Come near
Outta here with that—you hear?
I don't want it winding up my leg
Using my hair as a nest
Crawling up my shoe! Yiiikes!
It's poison—look at its tongue.
It's poison poison poison—look at its tongue.
Tell me you're not . . .
Pink? It is pink? A pink slithery
Deadly poisonous . . . look at its fangs?
Not poisonous? Look at its fangs!
It's pink and it's not poisonous.
Really? Not p-p-p-ois . . .

SNAKE
You promise it's not P-p-poisonous . . . Okay my hands Are out . . . no I won't open my eyes Okay okay Wooooh Woooh Well look at that—A sweet little pink, pretty Nonpoisonous snake. A living soda straw An endless neck
One long finger Swimming through my hands. Hey there sweet snake.
Gimme a kiss
Ssssss.

Are they called buzzards
Because they buzz?
I mean I don't think a buzzard
Should go "peep"
But Buzz Buzz Buzz Buzz
Like a saw.
He's a creepy little guy. Almost
Bald like my Uncle Frank,
With a few spiked hairs
Like me.
Swollen sad eyelids
Like he doesn't
Want to get up.
Or has hay fever like Mattie.
Hey! Maybe that's why
His beak is so huge.

And he sneezes his baby
Buzzard face blue.
Should we call him a "sneezard"?
No.
(But that's a fine name for something.)
This baby buzzard fell out
Of a tree
And his sisters said "get out" and
"Stay out you freak!"
So right now this bald buzzard is blue
But in a few years
He'll make chopped liver
Out of you.
Eeeeeek!
Who wants a buzzard?
Buzz Buzz
Who wants a buzzard?
Buzz Buzz
With the beak of a hacksaw
And a heart full of peep.

Buzzard

A RAT?

Mrs. Finklestein wants a rat
"Yes I do, young man
No doubt of that."
A rat Mrs. Finklestein a big
White rat?
"Yes that's true young man
They're very sweet
When not raised on the garbage of the street.
Then their habits are disgusting
And they carry old tuna fish
On their feet."
But why not a dog or
Cat?
"Because I want a rat that's why
A rat
One that's calm; one that's older
One I can carry on my shoulder."
But Mrs. Finklestein, you're
Eighty-four!
"That's never stopped me before.

I just hiked a mountain,
Waxed the kitchen floor,
Danced the twist at the senior club,
And fiddled with the engine
On my fuel-injected Ford."
Are you afraid a rat
Might bite?
"He just might young man.
But for him it won't
Be so grand.

I taste like sand
I taste like liver and
Old refried beans.
I taste like Brillo and wet blue jeans."
Mrs. Finklestein wants a rat.
One to rub and one to pat.
Mrs. Finklestein—here's your rat.
"Good—I'll name him after my ex-husband
Nat."

Take the butterfly
Out of the jar
Out of the jar
Out of the jar.
Let the butterfly
Sail toward a *star*
Up in the air.
Unscrew the lid on
That glass.

Let the butterfly
Pass through your hands.
Fluttering butterfly
Flapping colored tissue paper wings
Swoosh let it fly.
Its colors are brighter
Against the *sky*.

You don't need
To see it up close.
Don't pinch its wings
Just let it go
By the newspaper stand

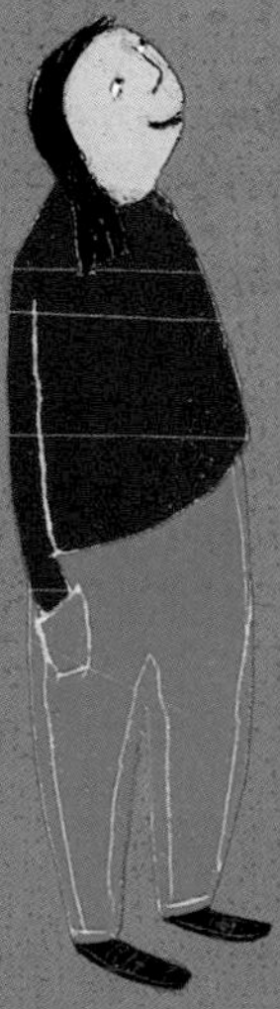

Butte

By the pizza store
Up up past the nose of the policeman's
Horse
And of course past the
Scaffolds and metal cranes
(Watch out for the windowpanes).
Up up flutter flutter
Flutter butterfly
Fly past the dishes and TV antennae
200 meters ahead of the cars.

Take the butterfly
Out of the jar
Out of the jar.
Let the butterfly
Sail toward a star.

COCKATOO

Heavy metal cockatoo
Get down!
Get down!
Get down!
With your big bad self!
My cockatoo's a rapper
And a heavy metal singer
Whatcha want whatcha want
Whatcha want from me
Baaybee?
My mother says
We can't keep him
Unless he lowers his volume
And learns some Natalie Cole.
I Love Rock and Roll!
I don't think he's going
To last in this abode.
Can you take the heat?
Have you got it bro?
He learned his stuff from the radio.
Get down! Get down!
Get down!
With your big bad self!
Funky funky funky funky!

Chick-en! Let's cook a chicken!
Maybe you could find
Him a home
With a drummer
Or a carpenter
Who hammers all day long.
Or a hard-of-hearing couple
Who live way back in a forest in another hemisphere.
Play it for me baby
Play it for me baby
Yessa! Yessa! Yessa!
Heavy Metal Cockatoo!
(Murder on the ears.)

PUFFY PRINCE POODLE

Puffy Prince Poodle is a champion.
His proper name is
Lord Cottonbatton Alfred Schmitz Runs Like a Reindeer Lord Prince Cottonbatton Alfred Schmitzy the 3rd.

Puffy Prince Poodle
Won't say a word.
Comes from a famous line of hoity-toity
show dogs.

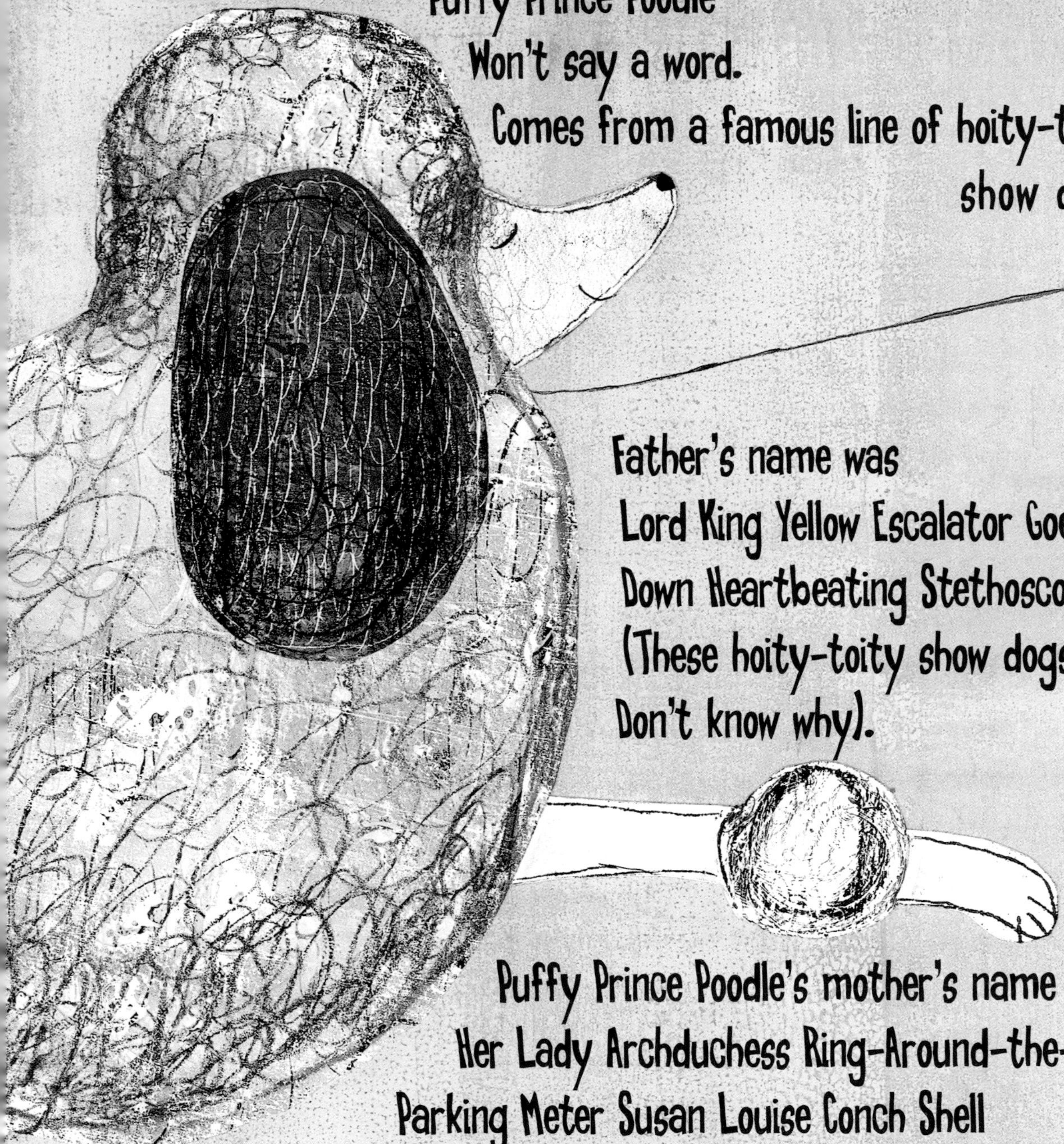

Father's name was
Lord King Yellow Escalator Goes
Down Heartbeating Stethoscope Sam
(These hoity-toity show dogs have long names;
Don't know why).

Puffy Prince Poodle's mother's name was
Her Lady Archduchess Ring-Around-the-Rosy
Parking Meter Susan Louise Conch Shell
It's a Great Day O'Hara.
And finally
Puffy Proper Prince Poodle's grandma's
Name was
Mrs. Cohen.
Mrs. Cohen?

Coooo

Shh—there's a dove.
She's white and clear
But she's not free.
Did she fall out of a tree?
Coooo dove
Coooo sweet dove
Did you know your name
Rhymes with "love"?
Coooo dove
Coooo sweet dove
Do you know
You're supposed to mean "peace"?
Coooo dove
Coooo sweet dove
Your wings are beginning to
Lift.
Coooo dove
Coooo sweet dove
You're someone's
Summer gift.

Tiny Turtles

Sid gets a call from Chinatown.
A truck full of turtles bumped on a pothole.
Now there're these tiny tiny turtles all around.
Running running running in the rain and the cold.

Tiny tiny turtles from the bumpy turtle truck.
Pretty painted shells so they can be sold as souvenirs
Right in front of Szechuan Chow Luck.
Tiny tiny turtles crying tiny tiny tears.

So Sid gets us started. We scramble on our knees
While the tourists around eat Chinese.
And skitter skitter skitter clomp and zoom
They may be tiny, but they sure can move.
Oops I got six in my pocket ti ti ti ti ti.

湖南又一村
HUNAN
RESTAURANT
大旺
BIG WONG
RESTAURANT
神天茶餐廳
TEA
PARLOR
PEKING DUCK

Wow three crawled into my sock, oh no.
Okay I gotchoo and I gotchoo and I gotchoo too.
Now I'm a tiny turtle boat.

Take the tiny turtles back to Sid's store
Scrub them and feed them, sing them tiny tunes.
No no no no they will not be sold.
No more, tiny turtles, no more.

DOG

Llama

Ho hum I'm just so . . .
Oh really to whom am I talking?
You seem very silly compared to well . . .
Me . . .
Ho ho ho hum
Don't you think my coat is
Quite extraordinaire?

I'm sure you're very jealous
But I don't care.
Ho hum ho hum
Yes I'm rahther glorious
Yawn yawn rahther brilliant.
I find you rahther boring ho hum. Rahther.
Your neck's not as long and sleek

As mine
Nor is your forehead
As fabulously regal ho hum ho hum.
You're blasé rahther blasé.
What does that mean?
I couldn't say.
I think it's French
For "nerd" or "geek."
I'll have my butler
Look it up
When he's done brushing my rahther magnificent coat.
Ho hum ho hum
I know you'd like to try it on
But–
No you dumb one
I'd rahther you not.
Ho hum ho hum
I'd rahther you go play
Elsewhere.

Guinea Pig

Fuzz ball
Just don't move at all.
Sits there like my mother's
Purse.
Wait—I think it twitched
Its nose.
Wait a minute wait a minute
Wait a minute wait a minute
It's moving I think.
Yeah it's sort of
Sloshing along
Like a toy in a tub
Facedown clumsy.
Where're its feet?
Does this model
Come with feet?
Fuzz ball
It stopped again.
Doesn't have a lot of breath I guess.
Gonna be a long day.
Watching this little
Fuzzy ball. Hmmm.

THE RABBIT'S LIFE

Chomp chomp
Chomp chomp
Twitch twitch
Chomp chomp
Carrot celery
Chomp snap
Lettuce tear crunch
Corn
Zziza zziza
With the teeth
Hop
Chomp chomp
Twitch snap zizzard
Crunch
Hop
Snuggle twitch
Slurp water slurp
Chomp chomp slurp
Snuggle snooze
Snooze

TARANTULA TIME

I'll grantcha
A tarantula's a
Very scary spider.
Hair on her back
And it's a fact
There's poison stored
Inside her.
But what a web this lady spins–
Windows lined with silken thread.
And any bug that wanders by
Ends up very dead.

I'll grantcha
A tarantula is
Huge and fat and black.
And don't forget the worst of it.
All those thick hairs on her back.
But if I could keep one jar
A jar that's closed up tight
I'd feed her beetles, bugs, and flies.
She'd scare away my
Bad dreams.

Thieves would run backward
Shaking with fear–
"Look there's a tarantula!
Let's get out of here!"

Lobster

I'm not gonna adopt
A lobster.
I won't have a lobster as a pet!
You boil lobsters
You broil lobsters
You barbeque lobsters.
There's no pet underneath
That shell.
It's a shell. It's red.
It clanks, it scrapes.
Its claws look like
Wire cutters, a pair of pliers.
Scratch clank scrape squeak
I don't want scratchy

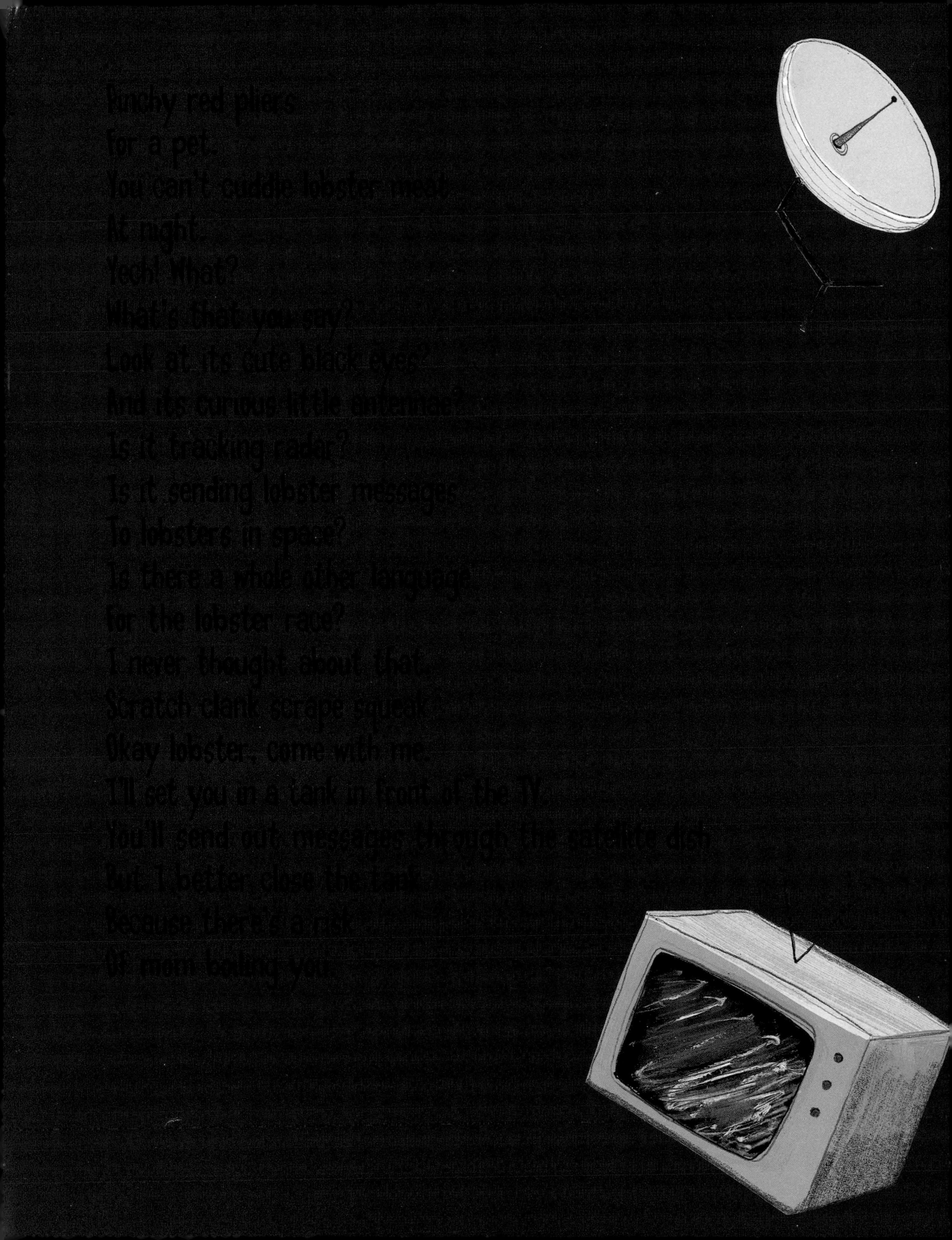

Punchy red pliers
For a pet.
You can't cuddle lobster meat
At night.
Yech! What?
What's that you say?
Look at its cute black eyes?
And its curious little antennae?
Is it tracking radar?
Is it sending lobster messages
To lobsters in space?
Is there a whole other language
For the lobster race?
I never thought about that.
Scratch clank scrape squeak.
Okay lobster, come with me.
I'll set you in a tank in front of the TV.
You'll send out messages through the satellite dish.
But I better close the tank
Because there's a risk
Of mom boiling you.

Combination Plate

This mutt doesn't know
Who he is.
He's part shepherd, part collie,
Part terrier, Chihuahua—
He's bulldog, bloodhound, and poodle
And shih tzu.
He's confused about his bark
Arf Roof Bark Oof Roof
Ratrr or Roo
He's got some wolf or fox in him too.
Does he go grr or rrrr
Or snarl or noof or ahwoooo!
Can he run as fast as greyhounds do?
Does he wag his tail?
Does he have a tail?
He keeps forgetting
And spins in circles trying to
Catch it . . .
(If it's there.)
Zoom tail! Zoom no tail!
Zoom tail! Zoom no tail!
He's part cocker spaniel,

Pointer, part Pekingese
So does he chase squirrels up a tree
Or act real ta ta ta and fussy?
There are so many parts of him
They can't seem to agree.
His nose is pushed in pulled out
Hooked up and down
He's lean but fat and yellow, black,
And brown.
He's Afghan and chow chow, Maltese
And pug.
Well we know one thing he knows how to hug and
Get what he wants
Ahwoooo!
Hey mutt . . . or Miss
(What if he's a "miss"?)
You're a complicated recipe
A combination plate
But what a personality.
You're like a whole family
Sleeping in one bed.
Ahwoooo!

Fish look dumb
Sorry but they do
Mouths always half open
A-duuuh
Like they got a nose cold.
Fish don't get old
Fish don't get young
Ain't got no fingers
Ain't got no thumbs
They're too dumb.
A-duuuh
Lotsa pretty colors
I'll grant you that
But those big poppy eyes
Got no sad or glad.
A-duuuh
They're cold as—well, fish
They don't feel nothin'
Empty inside.

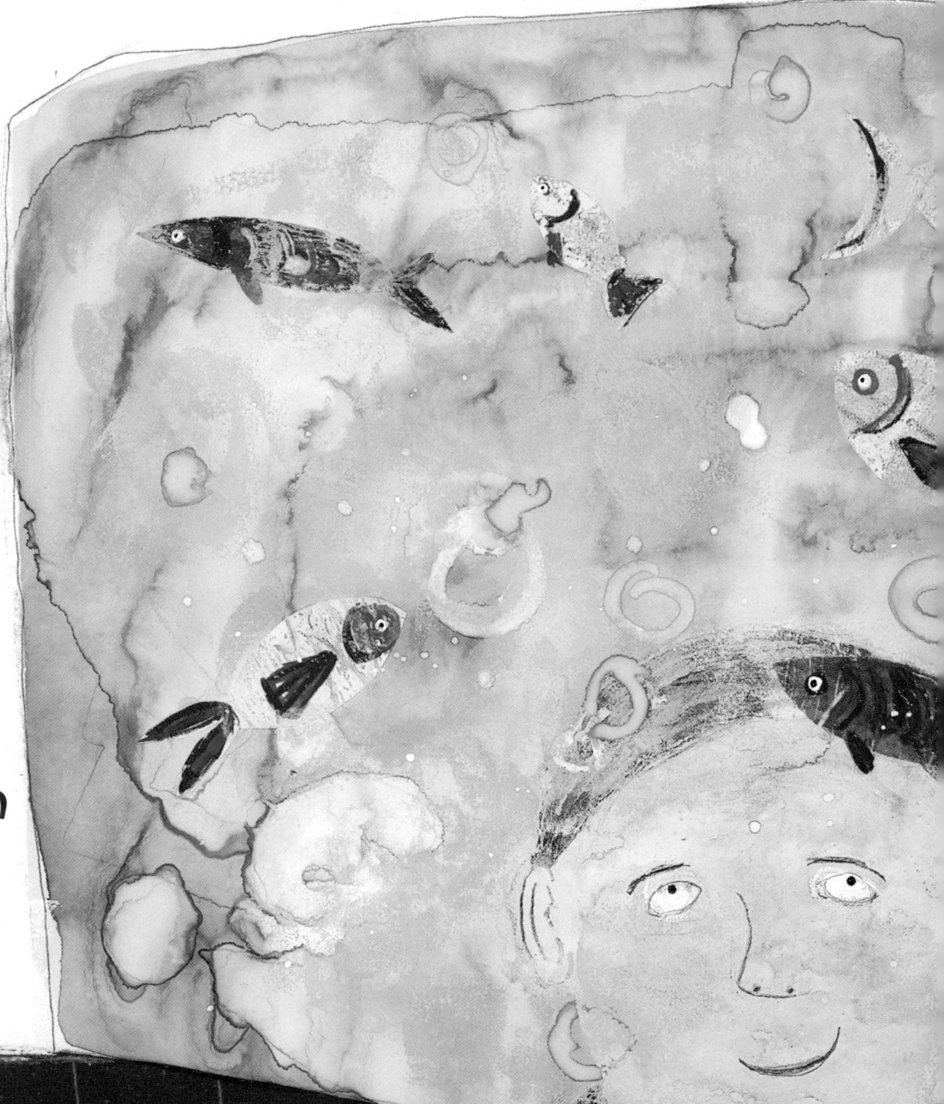

FISH

Might as well be filled
With stuffing.
They move real beautiful
I'll grant you that
But they're not smart enough to
Swim alone.
They swim in gangs called
Schools.
They wanna be in
Schools?
A-duuuh
Fish are real
Quiet
No chirps or bark.
Don't care about nothing
Unless it's a shark.
A-duuuh
And you'd be crazy
To adopt a shark.
A-duuuh

My Vagabond Zoo
CLOSED

Sidney pats
The rat and cat
And calms the
Llama with his palm
Puts a cover on the cockatoo's
Cage and then feeds some
Arugula to the rabbit
Tugs the tail on the
Pig puts the big
Bad boa back into
His basement corner
Takes the scary
Tarantula listens to
The hisses that the other
Snake makes.
Has the iguana gone
Under the house?
Nooo-good.
Gives the mouse
Some cheese
Leaves the turtle
In its shell
A banana for the not-
So-well-behaved chimpanzee.
Whispers to the butterfly,

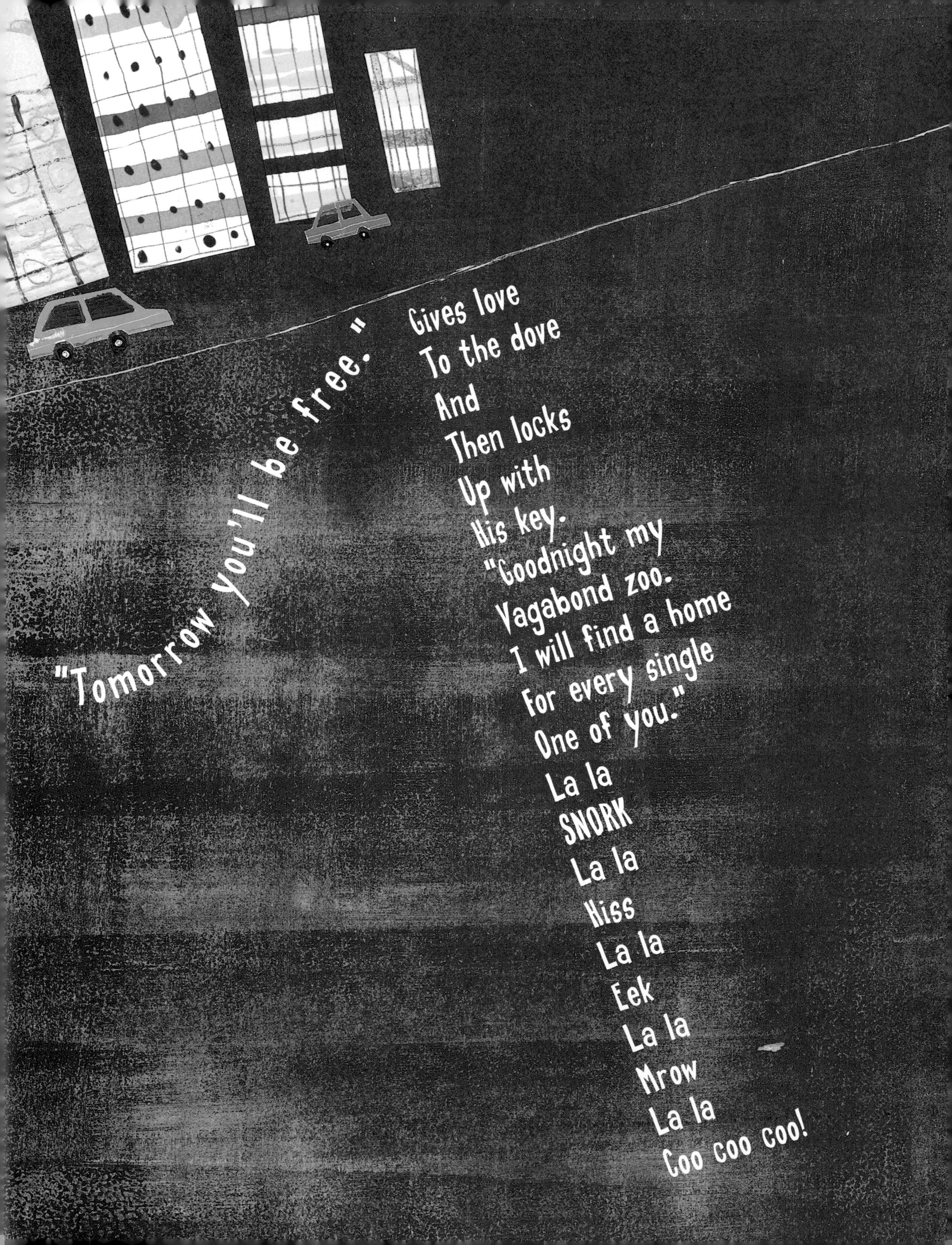
"Tomorrow you'll be free."
Gives love
To the dove
And
Then locks
Up with
His key.
"Goodnight my
Vagabond zoo.
I will find a home
For every single
One of you."
La la
SNORK
La la
Hiss
La la
Eek
La la
Mrow
La la
Coo coo coo!